# A Woman's Journal

# A Woman's Journal

*Helping Women Recover*

A Program for Treating Addiction

Stephanie S. Covington

JOSSEY-BASS
A Wiley Company
www.josseybass.com

Published by Jossey-Bass
A Wiley Imprint
989 Market Street, San Francisco, CA 94103-1741    www.josseybass.com

Jossey-Bass books and products are available through most bookstores. To contact Jossey-Bass directly call our Customer Care Department within the U.S. at (800) 956-7739, outside the U.S. at (317) 572-3986 or fax (317) 572-4002.

Jossey-Bass also publishes its books in a variety of electronic formats. Some content that appears in print may not be available in electronic books.

Text design by Paula Goldstein.

ISBN: 0-7879-4610-9

Printed in the United States of America
FIRST EDITION
*HB Printing*          10 9 8 7 6

# Contents

# Appendix: Additional Recovery Resources  121

# A Woman's Journal

# Introduction

## About This Program

I have been treating chemically dependent women for over twenty years. In that time, we have learned a great deal about how women grow and develop and about the unique needs of women in recovery. I have incorporated that knowledge into this program. Although the program is designed for women who abuse alcohol and other drugs, much of the material can be helpful to any woman.

*Helping Women Recover* addresses issues that many women struggle with, especially if they are abusing alcohol or other drugs. Each woman's path of healing is unique, but most of us find that it involves discovering our true selves, connecting in healthy relationships with others, understanding our sexuality, and gaining some spiritual connection. Recovery is like a spiral upward, away from a life that revolves around the objects of addiction (alcohol or other drugs, food, sex, and so forth), and outward into ever-widening circles of freedom, self-knowledge, and connection with others.

# The Spiral of Addiction and Recovery

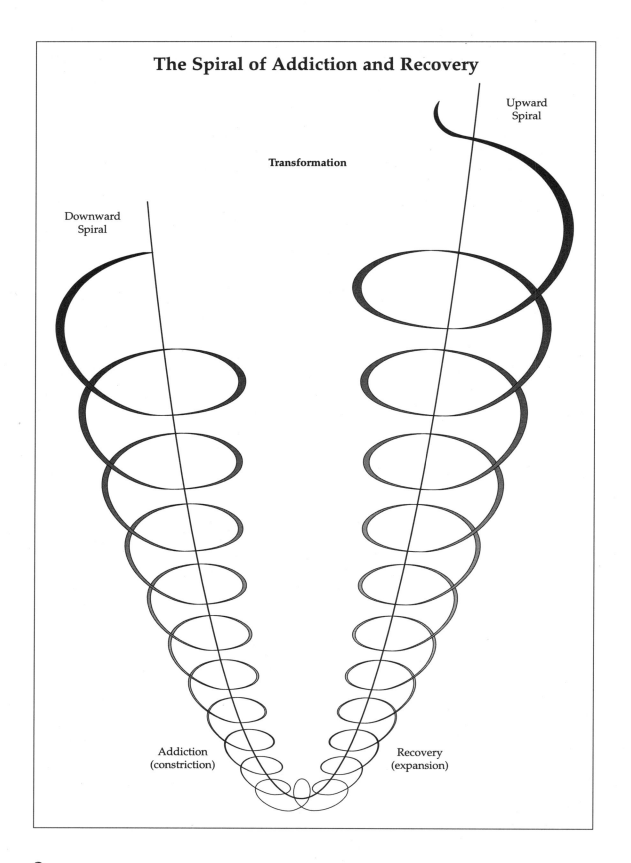

Transformation

Downward Spiral

Upward Spiral

Addiction (constriction)

Recovery (expansion)

Although this program may be used one-on-one with a counselor, in most cases you will be meeting with a group of other recovering women who will be traveling companions on your journey. You will attend seventeen meetings with the other members of your group. With them, you will have new experiences and learn new ways of looking at the world. Your group will be led by a group facilitator, a woman who has experience with the journey of recovery. She will serve as your tour guide. She will offer you insights and suggestions about the things, thoughts, and feelings that you may experience on your journey.

The program is organized into four modules: Self, Relationships, Sexuality, and Spirituality. These are the four areas that women identify as the triggers for relapse and the areas of greatest change in their recovery. Within the four modules, specific topics are covered, including

- Self-esteem
- Sexism
- Family of origin
- Relationships
- Interpersonal violence
- Sexuality and abuse
- Meditation and relaxation

Awareness is the first step toward change. When you become aware of your substance abuse, you can decide to begin recovery. When you become more aware of yourself and your relationships, you can make changes in your life. So the journey is about discovery as well as recovery. Healing takes place when you think and act differently, connecting with all parts of yourself—your inner self, your outer self, your sexual self, and your spiritual self.

# This Journal

A journal is a book for recording the experiences of a journey. Using this journal will help you to reflect on and record what you learn, think, and feel as you travel the road to recovery with your group. This journal contains

- Some of the exercises you will do during the group meetings
- Summaries of information that you will receive in meetings
- Questions and exercises for you to do as reflection after meetings

Space is provided in this journal for you to make notes about what you are thinking and feeling and what you discover about yourself and life as you go through this program. Recording your insights will help you to become aware and stay aware of them. Sometimes you will use your journal to make notes during group meetings. In addition, your journal contains illustrations and diagrams that you will discuss during the meetings. It also includes a summary of the material covered in each meeting. The summaries and your notes will help you to remember what you discussed. If you cannot remember what a diagram or something in the summary means, you can ask about it at the next meeting.

Finally, this journal contains questions and exercises for you to complete at the end of group meetings—or, if possible, between meetings. You will spend some time individually recording your thoughts and completing the brief exercises. These exercises are not work that you have to do in order to pass a class. There are no right or wrong answers, no "shoulds" or "oughts," and your reflections and responses will not be checked or graded. You do not need to worry about your handwriting or spelling. This journal is for you—a tool to help you to pursue your own growth and recovery.

You probably can do most of the exercises in a half hour, but it is fine if you also want to make notes or just review your progress. You probably will have insights into areas you haven't thought much about before. If you like to draw, feel free to draw your responses instead of, or in addition to, using words.

There will be opportunities during some group meetings for you to share things you have written in your journal. You can share what you want and keep the rest private. These times of sharing are chances to connect with the other members of your group.

The group meeting is a safe place, but you may be concerned about keeping your journal private. If you are not certain that others will respect your privacy, you can ask the facilitator to help you find ways to keep your journal safe between group meetings.

## Your Journey

I hope that this journal becomes a personal record of your recovery, one that you will treasure years from now, when you can look back to your time in the group and be proud of what you have accomplished. The reason for the creation of this program is my desire to see women like you recover and heal in a nurturing and supportive environment.

This program is a beginning for you—the beginning of your healing and recovery. It will take time for you to deal with the trauma of your past and integrate what you are learning. It takes time to learn, to recover, to change, and to move on. And when you have completed this program, you will see that it is just the beginning of a new life, one that includes ongoing recovery and ongoing learning about who you are, what you want, and what you can do.

I wish you the best.

*La Jolla, California*                                                                  Stephanie S. Covington
*December 1998*

# Module A
# Self

# Defining Self

## Program Ground Rules

At the beginning of Session 1, your facilitator will explain some ground rules for the group meetings. When everyone agrees to the ground rules, the sessions will have the most benefit for all group members. The ground rules are listed below for your reference.

1. **Attendance**   We're all committing to show up at all the sessions. Your commitment to attend regularly helps to stabilize the group and creates an environment of mutual support. If you must miss a group meeting, please let the group leader know before that meeting.

2. **Confidentiality**   No personal information revealed in this room is to be repeated outside the room. We need to know that we can trust one another, and there can be no trust if information about a group member is given to outsiders, or if group members gossip about one another outside the group. There are two exceptions to this rule of confidentiality: (1) the facilitator may have to communicate with other members of your treatment teams as part of your ongoing care; and (2) she is required by law to break confidentiality when a member's personal safety or the safety of another person is at stake. You, as a group member, will be responsible for maintaining confidentiality among your group.

3. **Participation**   Everyone should have a chance to join in the discussion. It is not helpful if some people dominate the conversation and if others remain silent. Also, please share all remarks with the whole group. Your comments, questions,

and opinions are of interest to all members, and side remarks from one individual to another tend to distract and divide the group. Sometimes your facilitator will ask a question and want everyone to respond. We would all like to hear what you have to say. However, if you are unwilling to talk about a particular subject, you have the option to "pass."

4. **Honesty**   We're here to tell the truth. The facilitator will be frank about herself. Nobody will pressure you to tell anything about yourself that you do not want to talk about, but if you do talk, tell the truth about where you have been and how you feel. It will be more helpful if you talk about your personal experiences, rather than about people in general.

5. **Respect**   When you tell the truth about what you think, please do so in a way that respects others in the group. That means no criticizing, judging, or talking down to anyone. If you think that someone is showing disrespect to someone else, please say so respectfully. We all need to know how we are coming across. Also, please let people finish what they're saying before you jump in. If someone is dominating the conversation, the facilitator will referee so that everyone gets a chance to talk. You might feel uncomfortable or angry at some point and not want to participate, but part of respect is agreeing not to derail the group for your personal agenda. You have the right to remain silent until you can participate according to the ground rules.

6. **Questions**   There are no dumb questions. Ask whatever is on your mind. Please respect one another's honest questions.

7. **Task**   We're here to talk about a program of recovery. Please try to stick to that topic. If we start to go off-task, the facilitator will direct us back to the topic at hand. If you think that we're getting off the topic and she is not doing anything about it, or if you think that she is headed off on a tangent, please feel free to refocus us.

8. **Punctuality**   We'll start on time and end on time. The times of our group meetings are _____.

In your group meeting you began the process of looking at yourself and answering the question, "Who am I?" This task will take you on a journey *inward*: exploring your inner feelings, thoughts, and beliefs. It will also take you on a journey *outward*: taking a new look at your relationships and the roles you play in the world.

# Who Are You?

As women, most of us have been taught to think of ourselves in terms of our roles as daughters, mothers, wives, relationship partners, employees, and so on. There is nothing wrong or bad about this—in fact, our connections with others tell us much about who we are. However, our roles do not tell the whole story about who we are. In recovery it is important to develop our relationships with others—our outer selves—and our relationship with our inner selves—our feelings, attitudes, and beliefs.

We are often uncomfortable focusing on "I" and worry about being "selfish." "Selfish" means focusing on ourselves without regard for others. However, in avoiding selfishness, we often become self-less; that is, we have no sense of our selves at all. Recovery is a time for learning about the self and healing the self. Perhaps you can begin to think of this time of focusing on yourself as being self-full: neither self-less nor selfish. Your work in the group will help you to develop a more complete, whole picture of yourself.

The questions in this section of your journal will help you to remember what you discussed and how you felt during your first group session.

## *Reflections*

1. When you talked in the group about how people would have described you when you were ten years old, what did you remember? Did you learn anything new about yourself? Write down what you remembered and what you learned from that. You also may write about what you felt when you told the group how someone would have described you.

2. When the question, "Who am I?" was discussed, what did you say? Take a few moments to write your response.

3. You may want to refer to the Possibilities Page (page 14) and check or circle any of the words there that may help you to answer the "Who am I?" question.

4. What qualities or characteristics of the other women in the group did you notice? Write down your observations. (You can note what you wrote on their sheets or things you want to write on their sheets or slips of paper during the next group session.)

5. Following the Possibilities Page is a page headed, "Who Am I?" In the space provided, and over the course of your work with the group, you can record all the insights about yourself that you gain from this program. Write things that you learn in group meetings, things that you learn from what the other women write on your sheet, things that you learn from this journal, and any other thoughts and feelings you have between meetings.

   Right now, on the "Who Am I?" page, write what the other group members wrote on your individual sheet that is hanging in the group meeting room or on your slips of paper.

6. Next, transfer to your "Who Am I?" page any feelings, beliefs, or qualities about yourself that you wrote down under question 2 above.

7. When you have completed question 5, look at the Possibilities Page again. If you see there any feelings, beliefs, or qualities that you would like to add to your list, do so. Then begin to make sentences on pages 16 and 17 that describe who you are. You can try to have at least twenty sentences by the last group session.

8. If you have any thoughts or feelings about how your addiction has affected the way you feel about yourself, please note them here.

# Possibilities Page

| Feelings | Beliefs | Qualities |
| --- | --- | --- |
| angry | honesty | sense of humor |
| joyful | importance of family | dependable |
| sad | loyalty | sincere |
| anxious | hard work | good natured |
| thoughtful | monogamy | trustworthy |
| nervous | God | smart |
| happy | save the earth | compassionate |
| afraid | save money | streetwise |
| amused | stay young at heart | gentle |
| hurt | motherhood is fun | strong |
| bitter | life is tough | creative |
| jealous | expect the best | survivor |
| calm | you are what you eat | wise |
| lonely | anger is dangerous | funny |
| mad | safe sex | warm |
| contented | reincarnation | honest |
| miserable | don't trust the government | passionate |
| disappointed | think before you speak | calm |
| pleased | trust your friends | sensible |
| overjoyed | better safe than sorry | energetic |
| discouraged | full of ideas | |
| depressed | good with words | |
| relieved | good with pictures | |
| glad | good with numbers | |
| disturbed | good at making things | |
| embarrassed | good listener | |
| furious | | |
| grateful | | |

# Who Am I?

*Your thoughts and feelings about yourself: Include things that you learn from what the other women write on your sheet (or slips of paper).*

**Examples:**

*I'm street smart.*

*I'm a person that people like to confide in.*

*I'm a survivor.*

*I am full of good ideas.*

*I'm often nervous.*

*I'm lonely.*

*Right now I feel better than I have in a long time.*

*I believe that life is tough, but I can make it.*

1.

2.

3.

4.

5.

6.

7.

8.

9.

10.

11.

12.

13.

14.

15.

16.

17.

18.

19.

20.

# Recovery Scale

Please take a few moments to mark the degree to which you do each of the following things. You can make an "X" or a circle on each line to indicate your response.

   You will complete this form again at the end of this module on Self to see how you have changed. You will not have to compare your answers with anyone else in the group, nor will you be judged on how well you are doing. This is not a test, but an opportunity for you to chart your own progress in recovery.

|  | Not at All | Just a Little | Pretty Much | Very Much |
|---|---|---|---|---|
| 1. I keep up my physical appearance (nails, hair, bathing, clean clothes). | | | | |
| 2. I exercise regularly. | | | | |
| 3. I eat healthy meals. | | | | |
| 4. I get restful sleep. | | | | |
| 5. I go to work/school (or I complete tasks). | | | | |
| 6. I can adapt to change. | | | | |
| 7. I keep up my living space. | | | | |
| 8. I take constructive criticism well. | | | | |
| 9. I can accept praise. | | | | |
| 10. I laugh at funny things. | | | | |
| 11. I acknowledge my needs and feelings. | | | | |
| 12. I engage in new interests. | | | | |
| 13. I can relax without drugs or alcohol. | | | | |
| 14. I value myself. | | | | |

# Session 2

# Sense of Self

We can think of our lives as journeys from birth, to where we are now, and to where we will be in the future. The landmarks of our journeys are

- *People* whom we have encountered along the way (mothers, teachers, counselors, correctional officers)
- *Events* we have been involved in (one-time occurrences, such as births, accidents, or being arrested)
- *Experiences* we have had (isolation in high school, summers with grandmothers, living in institutions)

Part of exploring who we are today is to go back and look at the people, events, and experiences that have shaped us. Sometimes looking at the past can be painful. We have experienced a lot of things that we would rather forget. But remembering is important because if we are cut off from our pasts, we're cut off from parts of our selves. Also, examining our pasts can help us to identify things that we want to be different in the future. The good news is that we can make choices today that will improve our lives six months or a year from now. The past has shaped us, but it doesn't have to control us. We can shape our presents and our futures through the choices that we make now.

On the next three pages, list the people, events, and experiences that have played major roles in creating who you are today. You can write in words and phrases or draw pictures or symbols.

# People

Examples:

*my mom—a heavy drinker*

*the girls I hung out with in junior high school*

# Events

Examples:

*the birth of my first child*

*my sister leaving home*

# Experiences

Examples:

*moving around a lot as a child*

*hanging out with kids who knew the streets*

# *Reflections*

1. You took some time during your group meeting to list or draw the people, events, and experiences that have been most significant in your life. Now take another look at those lists and see if any more ideas come to mind.

2. Look back over the three lists you've created. Think about the strengths you've developed through the people, events, and experiences of your life. What are some of those strengths?

# Self-Esteem

Your self-esteem is the value you place on yourself. It is how you see yourself, and it affects who you are. Having high self-esteem doesn't mean having a big ego; it means that you know and value who you are.

Look at the picture. It illustrates the river of self-esteem. It shows how the messages we receive about ourselves feed into our views of ourselves, like streams feeding into a river. Those messages include things we've heard from others in the past and things we've told ourselves in the past. They also include things people are still saying to us and things we are still saying to ourselves. They include messages from television, radio, and movies, as well as from parents, boyfriends, partners, children, teachers, bosses, and others.

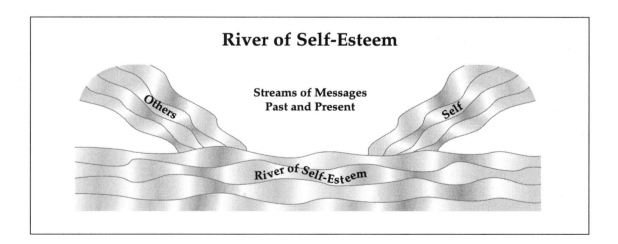

**River of Self-Esteem**

Others

**Streams of Messages Past and Present**

Self

River of Self-Esteem

All these messages either nourish or pollute the river of self-esteem. If you've heard positive things about yourself, such as "You are such a brave woman," you're likely to add that to your beliefs about yourself. On the other hand, if you've heard lots of negative things, such as "You're so stupid," or "You'll never be anything but a lousy drunk," you're likely to believe those things, and you'll probably develop very low self-esteem.

In your group session you made a collage that depicts the messages you have received about yourself from yourself and from others. In this journaling session, try to put into words what your collage pictured. Use the questions that follow to guide you.

## Reflections

1. What are some of the messages about yourself that you received in the past from other people?

2. What are some messages that you receive currently from other people?

3. What are some of the things that you said to yourself, about yourself, in the past?

4. What are some of the things that you tell yourself, about yourself, now?

5. How do these past and present messages affect the way in which you see your-self today?

6. What are some of the messages from others that you would like to stop hearing?

7. Which of the messages that you tell yourself would you like to stop?

8. Choose one of the following four affirmations:

❏ I am a worthwhile human being.
❏ I am a valuable woman.
❏ I like who I am.
❏ I have strengths that I can use in my recovery.

Write it below to complete this sentence:

The affirmation that I am going to use each day is _____

_____

Affirmation is a way to give yourself new messages about yourself—positive messages. When you repeat a positive message, it begins to undo a negative one that you may have been carrying around for a long time. Your thinking begins to change. You begin to see yourself differently and to feel differently about yourself.

Beginning today, say this affirmation *out loud* to yourself five times every morning and five times every evening, while looking at yourself in a mirror.

# Sexism, Racism, and Stigma

In your group session, you learned that a *stigma* is a visible characteristic that society interprets negatively. *Stigma* is Greek for "tattoo mark," and having a stigma is like having a tattoo that advertises something bad about you. In our society, just being female carries a stigma. Other aspects of a woman's identity also carry stigma in society—things such as race, class, sexual orientation, relationship status, age, size, and appearance.

The messages about women in our society, especially the ones related to stigma, strongly affect how women see themselves. In your group meeting, you listened to a fantasy in order to see how powerful those messages can be.

## *Reflections*

1. Recall how you felt when the fantasy was read in the group session. How did you feel when you imagined yourself to be a woman in that situation?

2. How did you feel when you imagined yourself to be a man in that situation?

3. Considering the things that you have learned, what messages that society sends about women would you like to ignore from now on?

4. Look at the lists "Act Like a Lady" and "Act Like a Man" on the two pages following your Reflections. They show the traditional roles that women and men have been given in our society.

    Notice that, according to this system, a "lady" is *being:* being polite, nurturing, submissive, and so on. Being a man is related to *doing.* Men are expected to hide their feelings or not to have them. They are supposed to be strong and in control, and they're never supposed to fail. Many men struggle under the pressure of having to live up to the ideal male image, just as women struggle under the pressure of conforming to their role. Both are limited if they're not allowed to be whole persons, capable of doing and feeling both "feminine" and "masculine" things.

5. Now look at the Power Chart on page 34. Circle all the items in each column that describe you. The items are in pairs: men/women; adults/young people; and so on. In some cases, you may circle just one item in the pair (you are either a man or a woman). In other cases, you may circle both items in the pair (you could be both a boss who has subordinates and a worker who has a boss over you). In other cases, you may not circle either item (for example, if you are neither a teacher nor a student).

6. Think about the items you circled on the Power Chart. In which areas do you have an advantage in our society? In which areas are you at a disadvantage?

*Areas of advantage or privilege:*

*Areas of disadvantage or oppression:*

7. How do you feel about your advantages or privileges?

8. How do you feel about your disadvantages or oppression?

# Act Like a Lady

**Ladies should . . .**

be polite

be sexy

be nurturing

take care of the house

be emotional

take care of the kids

be submissive

be superwomen

be dependent

put their needs aside

not be too smart

be clean

be pretty

be available to men

---

From *Men's Work: How to Stop the Violence That Tears Our Lives Apart* by Paul Kivel, published by Hazelden. Copyright © 1992 by Paul Kivel. Reprinted by permission of Hazelden Foundation, Center City, MN.

# Act Like a Man

| Men . . . | Men are . . . |
|---|---|
| yell at people | aggressive |
| have no emotions | responsible |
| get good grades | mean |
| stand up for themselves | bullies |
| don't cry | tough |
| don't make mistakes | angry |
| know about sex | successful |
| take care of people | strong |
| don't back down | in control |
| push people around | active |
| can take it | dominant over women |

From *Men's Work: How to Stop the Violence That Tears Our Lives Apart* by Paul Kivel, published by Hazelden. Copyright © 1992 by Paul Kivel. Reprinted by permission of Hazelden Foundation, Center City, MN.

# Power Chart

| Powerful Group | Less Powerful Group |
| --- | --- |
| men | women |
| adults | young people |
| bosses | workers |
| teachers | students |
| whites | people of color |
| rich | poor |
| Christians | Jews, Moslems, Buddhists |
| able-bodied | physically challenged |
| heterosexual | gay, lesbian, bisexual |
| formally educated | not formally educated |

# Recovery Scale

Please take a few moments to mark the degree to which you do each of the following things. You assessed yourself on this scale at the beginning of this module on Self. Please reassess yourself to see where you are now. You will not have to compare your answers with anyone else in the group, and no one will judge how well you are doing. This is not a test; it is an opportunity for you to chart your own progress in recovery.

|  | Not at All | Just a Little | Pretty Much | Very Much |
|---|---|---|---|---|
| 1. I keep up my physical appearance (nails, hair, bathing, clean clothes). |  |  |  |  |
| 2. I exercise regularly. |  |  |  |  |
| 3. I eat healthy meals. |  |  |  |  |
| 4. I get restful sleep. |  |  |  |  |
| 5. I go to work/school (or I complete tasks). |  |  |  |  |
| 6. I can adapt to change. |  |  |  |  |
| 7. I keep up my living space. |  |  |  |  |
| 8. I take constructive criticism well. |  |  |  |  |
| 9. I can accept praise. |  |  |  |  |
| 10. I laugh at funny things. |  |  |  |  |
| 11. I acknowledge my needs and feelings. |  |  |  |  |
| 12. I engage in new interests. |  |  |  |  |
| 13. I can relax without drugs or alcohol. |  |  |  |  |
| 14. I value myself. |  |  |  |  |

# Module B

# Relationships

# Family of Origin

Most women come into early recovery with a long history of disappointing relationships. Unhealthy relationships feed addictions, and healthy relationships provide the necessary environment for recovery. Our first relationship is with the family we grew up in—our family of origin. It is in our family that we first learn powerful messages about relationships. We often re-create relationships in our adult lives that are built on what we learned as children. Many of us did not grow up in healthy families; therefore, we may not know how to create a healthy relationship.

The next few group sessions focus on relationships and will help you to think about the relationships in your life. The group you are participating in is also providing you with a place to practice relationship skills.

In your fifth group meeting you talked about the families in which you grew up. The following cartoon of Family Trees shows how a family tree typically looked in the 1950s and the very different way one might look in the 1990s. In the 1950s, "family" usually meant a set of two parents who had children, then those children grew up, married, had their own children, and so on. Today, families are not so neat and tidy. Mothers are raising children as single parents. Grandparents are caring for grandchildren. In blended families, children may have two sets of parents, several sets of grandparents, and many stepsisters and stepbrothers. Some kids have parents who are not married or who are same-sex parents.

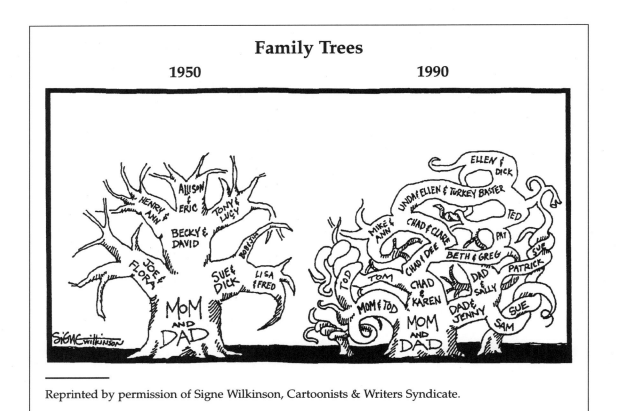

**Family Trees**

1950                      1990

Reprinted by permission of Signe Wilkinson, Cartoonists & Writers Syndicate.

In your group you discussed how children in stressful families end up playing roles in order to survive. Each of those roles carries with it certain positive and negative traits. Some of those traits are listed in the following chart.

# Positive and Negative Aspects of Roles

## Hero

| *Positive* | *Negative* |
|---|---|
| independent | fears rejection, confrontation |
| organized | perfectionist, fears failure |
| responsible | procrastinates |
| avoids risk taking | doesn't get personal needs met |
| powerful and in control | low self-esteem |
| focused, attentive | unable to play |
| loyal | immature "adult-child" |
| generous with praise | inflexible |
| successful | unable to label feelings |
| leader | guilt ridden |
| high achiever | feels inadequate |
| survivor | fears intimacy |
| motivates self and others | unreasonably high expectations |

## Scapegoat

| *Positive* | *Negative* |
|---|---|
| many friends | substance abuser |
| adapts easily | irresponsible |
| exciting life | manipulative |
| handles stress well | daredevil |
| traveler | passive aggressive |
| commands attention | rationalizes |
| fun loving | often on the hot seat |
| | lies, makes up alibis |
| | lacks close connections |

# Lost Child

| Positive | Negative |
| --- | --- |
| creative, imaginative | lonely, isolated, withdrawn |
| well-developed skills, manual dexterity | lacks social skills |
| well-read | feels invisible, excluded |
| good listener, observer | can be obsessed with self |
| spiritual | low self-esteem, distorted self-image |
| resourceful | sad, depressed |
| can work independently | mistrusts, blames others |
| nonconformist | fantasizes |
| enjoys solitude | inactive, indecisive |

## Mascot

| Positive | Negative |
| --- | --- |
| sense of humor | never taken seriously |
| charming | blames, projects |
| joyful | denies own feelings to maintain image |
| eases family tension, keeps the peace | dependent |
| playful, active | irresponsible |
| attracts attention | seeks attention |
| | deflects attention from real problem |

---

*Leaving the Enchanted Forest: The Path from Relationship Addiction to Intimacy* by Stephanie Covington and Liana Beckett, HarperCollins, 1988. Reprinted by permission of HarperCollins.

# Reflections

You probably have begun to think about which role was the main one you played as a child (your primary role) and which other one you used in certain situations (your secondary role). Use the following questions to reflect on what you discovered in the group.

1. How was your family of origin like the one that was sculpted in your group?

2. How was it different?

3. Go back to the chart, "Positive and Negative Aspects of Roles." Circle the traits that describe you today. If you would like to add any positive or negative traits to the list of those you circled, write them in.

4. What was your primary role when you were a child? (You may not have all of the traits of that role, but your primary role is probably the one with the traits you circled the most.)

5. What was your secondary role?

6. Your roles may have served you well when you were a child, but you do not have to be bound to them now. They probably do not fully express who you really are. Look over the traits you circled. Are there any that you would like to leave behind from now on? Write any changes you would like to make.

# Recovery Scale

Please take a few moments to mark the degree to which you do each of the following things. You will complete this form again at the end of this module on Relationships to see how you have changed. You will not have to compare your answers with anyone else in the group, nor will you be judged on how well you are doing. This is not a test, but an opportunity for you to chart your own progress in recovery.

|  | Not at All | Just a Little | Pretty Much | Very Much |
|---|---|---|---|---|
| 1. I share my needs and wants with others. | | | | |
| 2. I socialize with others. | | | | |
| 3. I stay connected to friends and loved ones. | | | | |
| 4. I nurture my children and/or loved ones. | | | | |
| 5. I am straightforward with others. | | | | |
| 6. I can tell the difference between supportive and nonsupportive relationships. | | | | |
| 7. I have developed a support system. | | | | |
| 8. I offer support to others. | | | | |
| 9. I participate in conversations with my family, friends, or co-workers. | | | | |
| 10. I listen to and respect others. | | | | |
| 11. I have clean and sober friends. | | | | |
| 12. I can be trusted. | | | | |

# Mothers

You had a chance during your group meeting to think about what your relationship with your mother, or mother substitute, was like when you were a child, a teenager, and an adult. You've thought about how you are like your mother and how you are different. You've also considered what your mother's life was like as a woman, not just in her role as mother. All of those questions may have stirred up some strong feelings for you, such as anger, sadness, longing, gratitude, or guilt.

## *Reflections*

Take about half an hour to think about what you would like to say to your mother. Write a letter to her without worrying about how she'll respond, because you aren't going to mail it. She's not here to evaluate how well you write or spell. So just write what you feel and think.

*Dear*

# Session 7

# Mother Myths

This page is for you to use in writing another letter. Your facilitator will explain it to you during the group session.

# Reflections

1. What are some of the things you and the group listed that mothers are supposed to do?

2. What are some of the expectations of fathers?

3. What did you learn from this exercise?

Sessions 6 and 7 emphasized your relationship with your mother or mother substitute because it probably has been the relationship that has most influenced the ways in which you relate to people today. However, other relationships also have been extremely important: those with your father or father substitute(s); your partner(s) or husband(s); and your key women friends. In the group session, you received a blank copy of the Relationship History Chart to fill out (and an extra copy in case you need it).

The chart that follows is included to provide an example, and sample answers are written in for the woman's key relationships.

Try to fill out your blank chart with at least five key relationships.

# Sample Relationship History Chart

|  | Mother | Father | Stepfather | Husband Al | Boyfriend Joe |
|---|---|---|---|---|---|
| Characteristics of person | Confusing Acted like a child Pushy | Happy Funny Funloving Flirty | Mean Macho Critical | Quiet Immature | Insecure Rigid Critical |
| Characteristics of relationship | Tangled Not dependable Inconsistent | Unreliable Playful | Abusive Neglectful Fearful | Both too young when married | Hostile |
| My role, My feelings | I was the adult Overwhelmed Scared | I felt attractive Daddy's "little girl" |  |  |  |
| Rewards of relationship | I was in charge | Got attention Had fun |  |  |  |
| Price of relationship | Grew up too soon | Felt uncomfortable |  |  |  |
| Involvement with chemicals or other addictive behaviors | Abused prescription drugs | Alcoholic | Abused alcohol and marijuana | Abused alcohol and marijuana | Drug addict |
| Response to addictive behaviors | Denial | Denial |  |  |  |

Adaptation of "Relationship History Chart," by Sue Evans, M.A., L.P. Reprinted by permission of Sue Evans.

# Relationship History Chart

|  | Mother | Father | 3) | 4) | 5) |
|---|---|---|---|---|---|
| Characteristics of person |  |  |  |  |  |
| Characteristics of relationship |  |  |  |  |  |
| My role, My feelings |  |  |  |  |  |
| Rewards of relationship |  |  |  |  |  |
| Price of relationship |  |  |  |  |  |
| Involvement with chemicals or other addictive behaviors |  |  |  |  |  |
| Response to addictive behaviors |  |  |  |  |  |

Adaptation of "Relationship History Chart," by Sue Evans, M.A., L.P. Reprinted by permission of Sue Evans.

# Session 8

# Interpersonal Violence

Domestic abuse is any exploitive or threatening behaviors intended to harm or exert power over another family or household member. Abuse can be emotional, physical, sexual, or economic. It includes, but is not limited to, the following:

**Emotional Abuse:** Playing mind games, calling someone names, constant criticizing, withholding approval or affection as punishment, public or private humiliation, abusing pets, threatening, manipulating, and blaming.

**Physical Abuse:** Pushing, slapping, kicking, choking, locking someone out of the house, threatening someone with a weapon, harassing someone to the point of physical illness, restraining (holding someone down, pinning the person's arms), depriving someone of sleep, biting, shaking, spitting, and giving someone a sexually transmitted disease.

**Sexual Abuse:** Raping, withholding sex and affection, unwanted or inappropriate touching, demanding sex after a beating or illness, sexual criticism, forcing sex in front of others, treating others as sex objects, and sadistic sexual acts.

**Economic Abuse:** Refusing to work or to share money, hiding the checkbook or credit cards, refusing to pay bills, taking back gifts, exploiting assets, using money to manipulate, and hiding money made through self-employment.

## Self-Soothing

When we are working through painful things, we need to have ways to comfort or soothe ourselves without using alcohol or other drugs. It's helpful to know ways to comfort ourselves before a time when we're in pain and need comfort. That is the purpose of the Self-Soothing Chart below. You will take some time in your group to think of ways to soothe yourself. Then take some more time on your own to think of more ideas.

The chart is divided into four squares because we need different ways to soothe ourselves in different situations. For instance, one strategy might work when we're alone but not when we are with people, and vice versa. Or some things will work during the day when we're alone but are not available at night. So we need ways to soothe ourselves in all four circumstances: alone or with people during the day and alone or with people at night.

You can come back to this chart later when you are feeling sad or anxious and need a way to soothe yourself. You also can add new ideas to your chart as you think of them.

## Self-Soothing Chart

| | Alone | with Others |
|---|---|---|
| Daytime | | |
| Nighttime | | |

# Reflections

Use the following questions and statements to reflect on your own possible experiences of abuse.

1. Put an X beside any of the kinds of abuse listed on page 53 that you have experienced. If you're not sure whether a situation was abusive, ask yourself these questions:

   Did I consent fully to this experience?

   Was this person betraying my trust?

   Was there violence, pain, restriction, force, or bodily harm?

   Did it feel like abuse to me?

2. If you have experienced any of these kinds of abuse, you may want to write them into your Relationship History Chart.

3. Not everyone has been abused by a member of her family or household. Still, most of us tend to minimize the abuse we have suffered, rather than making a big deal of it. It's helpful to look honestly at our past experiences, not so that we can feel bitter toward others, but so that we can understand the ways in which abuse has affected us and begin to heal. We have the power to start changing these effects from now on.

4. If you have been abused, how do you think your experience of abuse has affected your view of yourself?

5. If you have been abused, how do you think abuse has affected your relation-ships with other people?

How has it affected

- The ways in which you treat people?

- The people you choose to be close to?

- The ways in which you let people treat you?

6. What would you like to change about

• The way you perceive yourself?

• Your relationships?

# Creating Healthy Relationships and Support Systems

We all need people in our lives who provide emotional and practical support. We need people who will support our recovery. In your group you talked about supportive, growth-fostering relationships that help each person to achieve

- Growth
- Energy
- Empowerment
- Knowledge
- Self-worth
- Connections

   In contrast, with disconnections or unhealthy (or abusive) relationships, people feel

- Drained of energy
- Disempowered
- Confused
- Worthless
- Isolated

   The first illustration that follows is a sample of a Relationship Map. It shows one woman's relationships to people in her past and present, as well as her plans for relationships in the future. You will create your own map on the page that follows the sample. As you create your map, think about the qualities of healthy and unhealthy relationships.

After you have drawn your own map, take some time alone to write answers to the questions that follow the map.

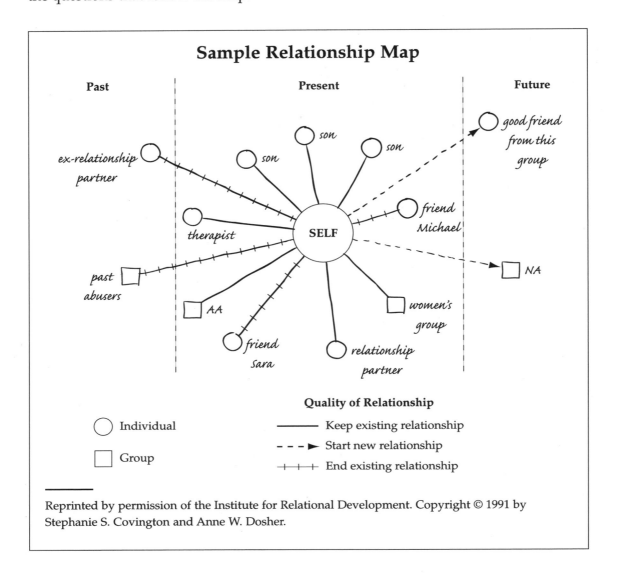

## Sample Relationship Map

Past                       Present                    Future

*good friend from this group*

*son*

*son*

*son*

*ex-relationship partner*

*friend Michael*

**SELF**

*therapist*

*past abusers*

□ *NA*

□ *AA*

*women's group*

○ *friend Sara*

○ *relationship partner*

### Quality of Relationship

○ Individual

□ Group

——— Keep existing relationship

- - - ► Start new relationship

+—+—+— End existing relationship

# Relationship Map

| Past | Present | Future |
|------|---------|--------|

**SELF**

### Quality of Relationship

○ Individual  ——— Keep existing relationship

☐ Group  - - - ► Start new relationship

+ + + + End existing relationship

Reprinted by permission of the Institute for Relational Development. Copyright © 1991 by Stephanie S. Covington and Anne W. Dosher.

# Reflections

1. As you look to the future, which of your current relationships do you want to continue and strengthen?

2. Which of your current relationships do you need to end because they will not support your recovery and help you to grow?

3. What new, supportive relationships do you want to pursue?

4. You have relationships not just with your family and friends, but also with the community and nation in which you live, and you have the power to make a difference in all those relationships. What kind of changes in your community or country would you like to work toward in the future? Following is a list of possible issues. Circle the one that is of most concern to you or add your own choices to the list.

- Sexism
- Racism
- Poverty
- Violence
- AIDS
- Other disease (specify)
- Alcohol and/or other drug abuse
- Children's welfare
- Child care
- Other (list your top choice):

5. What could you do as one step toward making a difference in the area you chose? For example, you might

- Write letters to your local government about a political issue that concerns you
- Sew for the AIDS quilt
- Write letters to a TV station or a manufacturer about an offensive ad
- Support or participate in a walk to raise money for a good cause

These are just a few ideas, and there are many other possibilities. You can make a plan to do something about the issue you circled in question 4. Don't limit yourself! Be creative. Even if you are living in a residential program (including a correctional institution), there are things you can do. Take your ideas back to your group. You have the power to make a difference in the world around you.

# Recovery Scale

Please take a few moments to mark the degree to which you do each of the following things. You assessed yourself like this at the beginning of this module on Relationships. Please reassess yourself to see where you are now. You will not have to compare your answers with anyone else in the group, and no one will judge how well you are doing. This is not a test; it is an opportunity for you to chart your own progress in recovery.

| | Not at All | Just a Little | Pretty Much | Very Much |
|---|---|---|---|---|
| 1. I share my needs and wants with others. | | | | |
| 2. I socialize with others. | | | | |
| 3. I stay connected to friends and loved ones. | | | | |
| 4. I nurture my children and/or loved ones. | | | | |
| 5. I am straightforward with others. | | | | |
| 6. I can tell the difference between supportive and nonsupportive relationships. | | | | |
| 7. I have developed a support system. | | | | |
| 8. I offer support to others. | | | | |
| 9. I participate in conversations with my family, friends, or co-workers. | | | | |
| 10. I listen to and respect others. | | | | |
| 11. I have clean and sober friends. | | | | |
| 12. I can be trusted. | | | | |

# Module C
# Sexuality

# Session 10

# Sexuality and Substance Abuse

There is much more to sexuality than just sexual behavior. Sexuality is an identification, a biological drive, an orientation, and an outlook. Sexuality involves our physical, emotional, psychological, and spiritual selves. One definition of healthy adult sexuality is "the physical, emotional, social, and spiritual parts of ourselves integrated into our identities and ways of living." Our sexuality includes our perceptions and feelings about ourselves as women and our perceptions and feelings about others. It involves how we act and with whom we act. Our sexuality reflects our energy, our life force. So sexuality is not just about having sex but involves many aspects of our selves, including how we feel about ourselves as women. So even if you are in a jail or a prison, where sexual behavior is controlled or against the rules, this is still an important area of life to explore.

We are all born sexual beings. Male babies have erections, and female babies have vaginal lubrication. Your sexuality develops over time, and it is influenced by your experiences and relationships. Sexuality is a lifelong process of development and discovery, a totality of who you are and how you are in the world.

Substance abuse affects you physically, emotionally, socially, and spiritually, so it's not surprising that addiction affects every area of your sexuality. Therefore, addressing and healing all aspects of your sexuality is important to your recovery.

In Session 10, you talked about what you learned as a girl about sexuality, including the negative messages you received from society about being a woman. You learned that many kinds of sexual problems are extremely common among substance-abusing women, including the lack of desire, arousal, lubrication, and orgasm, as well as painful intercourse.

You also learned that people sometimes confuse love, sex, and intimacy. We can confuse our longing for emotional connection with the desire for sexual contact. We can also trade sex for intimacy, giving up our bodies in order to feel close to someone.

Some women trade sex for drugs or money. Some use sex to manipulate others. Because many women have little power to get what they need or want, they may use their bodies as sources of power.

## Reflections

1. What were some of the messages you received in your family about sex and sexuality?

2. Think about the role-reversal exercise you did in the group. What did you learn from the guided fantasy about messages you have received from society about sexuality?

3. Many substance-abusing women are concerned about lack of orgasm, have shame about sexual activity, and fear having sex when they are clean and sober. What are some of your sexual concerns?

4. There will be four more sessions on sexuality in which you may raise any of these concerns. On the other hand, you may have some questions that you would prefer to discuss with your counselor privately. What questions would you like to discuss with your counselor?

5. The Sexual/Chemical Lifeline is a way to begin to see the relationship between your use of alcohol or other drugs and your sexual behavior. A sample lifeline appears on page 71. On the page after that is a blank chart. Chart your own lifeline, using a dotted line for your history of chemical use and a solid line for your sexual history. The horizontal baseline is marked 5, 10, 15, and so on. Those numbers represent your age. On the left side of the chart is a vertical line labeled +10, 0, and –10. Events that are pleasant experiences fall in the 0 to +10 range, from okay to really great. Painful events fall in the 0 to –10 range. The more painful the event, the closer it is to –10.

As you look back through your past to identify your sexual experiences, you may remember events you had forgotten, or you may be surprised at how painful some of your memories are. You may become aware of certain patterns, especially patterns between chemical and sexual activities. It's not uncommon to find that, as your substance abuse progressed, your sexual experiences became less pleasant. You also may find that incidents of certain sexual behaviors were associated with a lot of drug use, or that you had sexual relationships with drug suppliers.

By charting your Sexual/Chemical Lifeline, you can begin to become more aware of your sexual self while you were abusing alcohol and/or other drugs. Then you can start thinking about your sexual self in recovery and consider what changes you would like to make. Stop now and turn to the sample of Theresa's lifeline and then fill out your own on the following page. Then return to this page and answer the rest of the questions below.

6. Look over your completed lifeline. How did your substance abuse affect you sexually?

7. Now that your drug of choice is removed from your life, how do you envision your sexual self in the future?

**Theresa's Sexual/Chemical Lifeline**

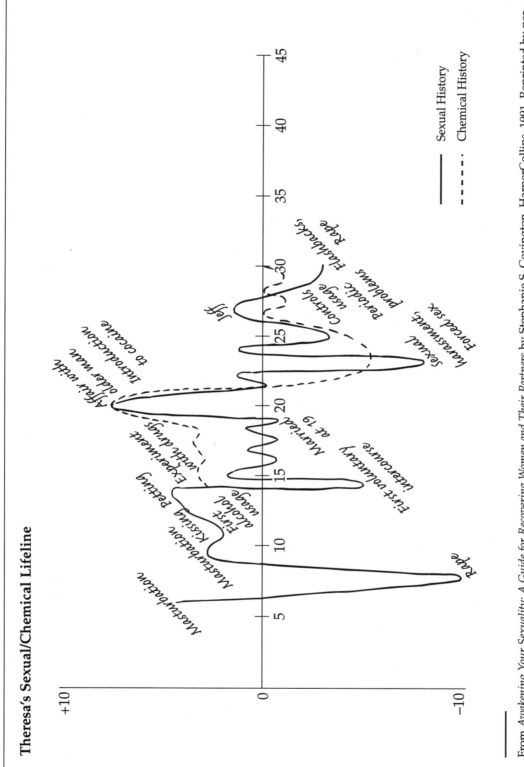

From *Awakening Your Sexuality: A Guide for Recovering Women and Their Partners* by Stephanie S. Covington, HarperCollins, 1991. Reprinted by permission of Stephanie S. Covington.

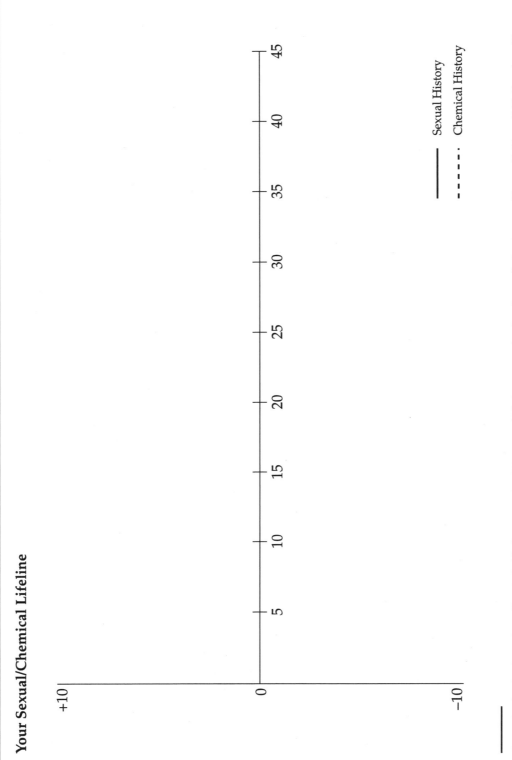

**Your Sexual/Chemical Lifeline**

+10

0

−10

5  10  15  20  25  30  35  40  45

——— Sexual History

- - - - - Chemical History

From *Awakening Your Sexuality: A Guide for Recovering Women and Their Partners* by Stephanie S. Covington, HarperCollins, 1991. Reprinted by permission of Stephanie S. Covington.

# Recovery Scale

Please take a few moments to mark the degree to which you do each of the following things. You will assess yourself like this again at the end of this module on Sexuality. This will provide an opportunity for you to chart your own progress in recovery.

If you are currently living in a correctional setting, some of the items may not be relevant at this time. You can cross them out or just not respond to them (but you may want to think about how you would like your life to be in the future, when you are released).

| | Not at All | Just a Little | Pretty Much | Very Much |
|---|---|---|---|---|
| 1. I know my body. | | | | |
| 2. I can talk to my counselor about sexual concerns. | | | | |
| 3. I can speak comfortably and appropriately about sex. | | | | |
| 4. I can keep my body safe. | | | | |
| 5. I accept my body. | | | | |
| 6. I can be affectionate with others. | | | | |
| 7. I am a sensual person. | | | | |
| 8. I can accept sexual pleasure from myself. | | | | |
| 9. I can accept sexual pleasure from my partner. | | | | |
| 10. I initiate making love. | | | | |
| 11. I can express my sexual desires to my partner. | | | | |
| 12. I enjoy making love. | | | | |

# Session 11

# Body Image

Most women today, even those who are considered beautiful, feel bad about some parts of their bodies. It might be their weight, height, hair color or type, the shape and size of their breasts, or the texture of the fat in their thighs. That's just part of living in a society that places enormous importance on how a woman looks and holds her to nearly impossible standards.

Our society tells us that young bodies are better than old ones, thin bodies are better than fat ones, bodies without the marks of pregnancy are better than those with stretch marks and scars, and light-skinned bodies are better than dark-skinned ones. Some of us do various things to our bodies in order to please ourselves or others: dieting, exercising, hair curling and straightening, painting, tattooing, and piercing. It's hard for many of us to accept our bodies as they are, especially when age, pregnancy, and other experiences change our bodies over time.

Substance abuse complicates the already complicated relationship that women have with their bodies. Many women who use alcohol or other drugs neglect their bodies. Others become obsessed with having perfect bodies. They may use drugs to manage their weight or to get over the negative feelings they have about their bodies. In criminal justice settings, many women feel especially disconnected from their bodies. Often there is high-calorie food or "junk food" in the commissary and limited opportunities for exercise. In addition, some women disconnect from their bodies—go numb—as a defense mechanism that helps them to survive incarceration.

Some women have bodies that have been numbed by the effects of alcohol and other drugs. Clean, sober bodies provide us with sensation and feeling. Many women confuse pleasurable sensations—the sensual—with sexual feelings. Sensuality has to do with bodily sensations, such as the pleasure of standing under a warm shower, the

75

feeling of wind blowing against your skin, the heat of the sun on your back, and the softness of a baby's skin. These feelings are sensual, not sexual. Some incarcerated women cut themselves off from sensuality because of the taboo against sexuality in criminal justice settings. A hug can be sensual or sexual, and if you have never had a nonsexual hug, you may need to learn to recognize the difference.

In early recovery, a woman's body may begin to have more feeling, as the numbness from alcohol and other drugs is eliminated.

Our bodies are part of us—so if we hate our bodies, we are actually hating ourselves. It is important for a recovering woman to learn to love, respect, and accept her body, whatever its size, shape, age, or type. It is also important for a woman to "get into" her body, to reconnect with it, to feel pleasurable feelings, and to have "embodied" experiences. This is a process that takes time.

## Exercise in Group Session

1. Following are two outlines of a woman's body. The first represents the front of your body, and the second represents the back of your body. Fill in these figures by marking them in one of three ways:

   • Mark the parts of your body that you like and feel satisfied with like this: + + + +.

   • Mark the parts you do not like, hate, or feel uncomfortable with like this: o o o o.

   • Mark the parts of your body that you feel neutral about with dotted lines (- - - -).

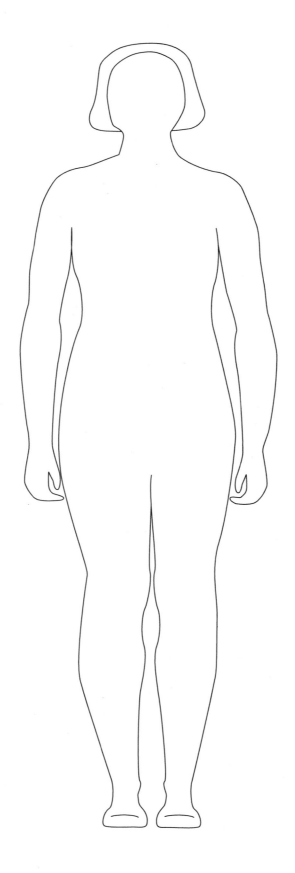

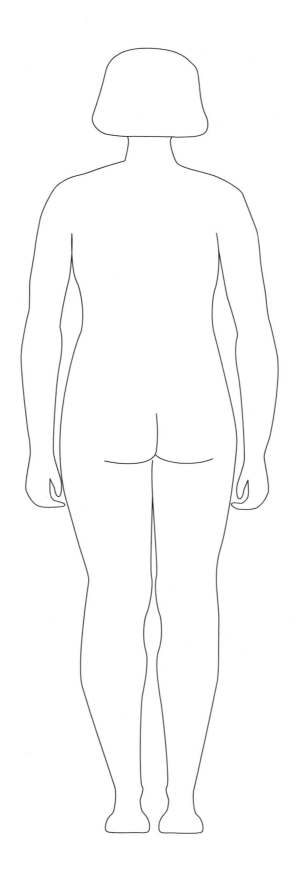

2. You have had a silent dialogue with some part of your body. When you are finished, please record here what you and your body said to each other.

The first part of the next section (items 1 through 6) is an exercise in which you look at your body in a mirror while you are undressed. If you live in a correctional setting, it may not be possible for you to do this exercise because of limited access to a mirror that you can use for this purpose. If you cannot complete the activity, go on to item number 7.

## Reflections

You can learn about your body by examining it in a mirror. If you find the idea of looking at yourself naked a little scary, you are not alone. Many women find it hard to look at their bodies without clothes on. If you find it hard to do this activity, be patient with yourself. You may have to do the exercise several times before you become comfortable in looking at your body. You can start by looking at one or two parts of your body. Every time you try the activity, add another part of your body or take a little more time. Try doing the exercise every day for a while, even if you can manage only a few minutes at a time. It will be easier to do this exercise with a full-length mirror, but if you do not have one, use the largest mirror you have and look at different parts of your body, in turn.

1. Find a time when you are alone and will not be disturbed. Take off your clothes, including your shoes.
2. Use the mirror to look at your back. Look at as much of yourself as you can manage. Try to really notice what you look like.
3. Use the mirror to look at your front. Again, look at as much of yourself as you can manage. Try to notice what you really look like.
4. When you have tried the exercise a few times and have begun to look at your body with a certain amount of comfort, you are ready for the next step: to begin to accept your body. Take a deep breath. As you breathe out, let go of the negative things you think about your body: your "tiny" breasts, "ripply" thighs, or "bad" skin. Say aloud to your reflection, "You're fine. I like you just the way you are. This body is mine and it's okay."
5. Now slowly focus on every part of your body, in turn, expressing love to every part, as you would to the body of a child whom you loved. Say good things out loud to your body. Thank her for what she does for you. You might thank your feet for helping you run, walk, and dance. You might thank your spine for allowing you to sit and bend over. You might thank your breasts for letting you know you're a woman, for giving you sexual pleasure, or for feeding your baby.

6. Write some notes here about how it felt to look at your body in the mirror.

7. In your group meeting, you took some time to have a conversation with your body. Choose another part of your body, or the same one, and continue that dialogue in writing. Start as you did in the group, by getting into a comfortable position and closing your eyes. Breathe in and out slowly for a while. Count to seven while you breathe in, and again to seven while you breathe out. Paying attention to your breathing helps you to increase your awareness of your body. It helps you to "get into" your body. Being conscious of your breath will help you to be more conscious of your body.

   Let your mind be like the calm water of a lake, and let go of any thoughts that come to you.

   Just let yourself relax for a few moments while you listen to your breath. Then picture in your mind the part of your body that you want to talk to.

   When you have a good picture of it, open your eyes and begin to write. Here are some questions to think about:

   • How do I feel about this part of my body?

- When did these feelings begin?




- What have others said about this part of me?




- Where did I get the idea of how this part of me should look?

Write the conversation like a script. It might go like this:

You:  I hate having bad skin. I hate that at my age I still get acne on my face, my back, and my chest.

Your skin:  It hurts me when you say I'm "bad." I want you to appreciate me.

You:  Why should I appreciate you? I'm embarrassed to wear anything that shows my chest or my back because of you.

Your skin:  But think about everything I do for you. Don't you know how much pain you have when even a little of me is torn away? I hold you together and protect you from things that would hurt you.

You:  But why can't you be pretty and perfect? I hate feeling ashamed for you to be seen.

Your skin:  Almost nobody has perfect skin. When did you start feeling ashamed of me?

Write your dialogue here:

# Sexual Identity

One aspect of the recovery process is figuring out your sexual identity. Your sexual identity is the integration of your inner self (feelings, thoughts, and beliefs) with your outer self (behavior and relationships).

Substance abuse can affect your behavior and confuse your understanding of your sexual identity, just as it confuses your sense of self in other areas. Most women start drinking or using other drugs as teenagers, at the time that they are beginning to explore their sexual attractions. Substance abuse often complicates this discovery process. For instance, a woman might feel attracted to other women, and, because she has learned to see those feelings as "bad," she might drink in order to cover up those feelings or to act on them. Another woman might find herself sexually involved with a woman while using drugs, but once she's clean, she may be afraid of this involvement or find only men attractive.

## *Reflections*

In our society, there are many negative and confusing messages about sexuality. You learn, for example, that you are "gay" or "straight" and that you can tell which you are by whether you have sex with men or with women. However, it's not that simple. Alfred Kinsey interviewed around ten thousand people about their sexual histories and charted their responses on a scale of 0 (exclusively heterosexual) to 6 (exclusively homosexual). Most people were between 1 and 5 on the scale.

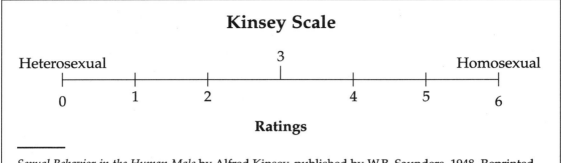

**Kinsey Scale**

Heterosexual ⊢—————————————————⊣ Homosexual

0    1    2    3    4    5    6

**Ratings**

*Sexual Behavior in the Human Male* by Alfred Kinsey, published by W.B. Saunders, 1948. Reprinted by permission of The Kinsey Institute for Research in Sex, Gender, and Reproduction, Inc.

1. You can do a brief exercise to see where you might fit on the scale by noting the number you would use to answer each of these questions:

- What's erotic to you—what "turns you on"? Do you find women's bodies erotic? Do you find men's bodies erotic? Do you find particular characteristics of men or women erotic? Are the lingerie ads in women's magazines erotic to you? Are the men's underwear ads erotic? Choose a number on the scale.

- Who are your fantasies about? Do your fantasies include both men and women? Do you fantasize about particular acts with either men or women? If you have fantasies only about one sex or the other, you would fall at one end of the scale or the other for this question. Choose a number to indicate where you are on the scale.

- Where do your strongest emotional attachments lie? Are you equally attached to both men and women? Who are your emotional bonds and connections with? Select a number on the scale that accurately reflects your emotional attachments.

- What is your sexual experience? Do you have sexual activity with both men and women? With whom have you had sexual activity? Choose a number that represents the variety of your sexual experiences.

Add up the numbers you have chosen for each of the four factors, then divide that total by four. The resulting number will tell you where you tend to fall on Kinsey's Sexual Identity Scale (Covington, 1991a). As most people fall somewhere between 1 and 5, only a small percentage of people are exclusively heterosexual or exclusively homosexual on all four of these factors. Some people in the middle of the scale have erotic attractions to or sexual relationships with both men and women and consider themselves bisexual.

People can answer the questions differently at different points in their lives. For instance, some women might put their identities at one point on the scale before they started drinking or using other drugs, at another place while they were actively drinking or using, and somewhere else when they became clean and sober and began to know themselves better. You may want to go back and answer the questions again, in terms of how you felt and what you did while you were using alcohol or other drugs. This will allow you to see if and how your sexual identity has shifted during recovery. Then, you may even want to answer the questions with an eye toward the future. This is an exercise to help you start thinking about parts of your sexual identity.

It is important for you to understand that it's not bad for you to find yourself anywhere on this scale. You do not have to be at one end or the other. If you find that you're more toward one end than the other, that may help you to define your sexual identity. It is not unusual for women to be confused about their sexual identities in early recovery. Use the questions below to reflect more on the subject of sexual identity.

2. In the group session, you discussed the messages that you received about lesbians and gay men when you were a child, an adolescent, and an adult. Write those messages here.

Child:

Adolescent:

Adult:

3. How did it feel for you to hear about and talk about lesbians in the group?

4. Does this session on sexual identity raise any issues for you that you want to discuss with your counselor? If so, what are they?

5. Do you feel fairly clear about what your sexual identity is, or is this an area that you would like to explore further in your recovery? (It's okay to feel that you're not ready to think about it now.)

6. Turn to the Sexual Attitudes and Behavior Scale on pages 90–91. Take a few minutes to circle the number on each scale that shows where you are now and to draw an arrow to where you would like to be. If you are incarcerated, some of the scale items may not be relevant to your life now, but you can still indicate where you would like to be on the scale. Some of these items may be important later in your life.

7. What issues does the Sexual Attitudes and Behavior Scale raise for you that you would like to discuss with your counselor?

# Sexual Attitudes and Behavior Scale

Circle the number on the scale that shows where you are now; draw an arrow to where you would like to be.

| Am unable to communicate verbally with partner about my sexual likes and dislikes. | | | | | | Am able to communicate verbally with a partner about my sexual likes and dislikes. | | | |
|---|---|---|---|---|---|---|---|---|---|
| 1 | 2 | 3 | 4 | 5 | 6 | 7 | 8 | 9 | 10 |

| Don't know what excites and turns me on sexually. | | | | | | Know what turns me on sexually. | | | |
|---|---|---|---|---|---|---|---|---|---|
| 1 | 2 | 3 | 4 | 5 | 6 | 7 | 8 | 9 | 10 |

| Am uncomfortable touching or looking at my body nude. | | | | | | Am very comfortable touching and looking at my body nude. | | | |
|---|---|---|---|---|---|---|---|---|---|
| 1 | 2 | 3 | 4 | 5 | 6 | 7 | 8 | 9 | 10 |

| Think that masturbation is a sin, is wrong, or I feel guilty about doing it. | | | | | | Think that masturbation is healthy and a way to care for myself. | | | |
|---|---|---|---|---|---|---|---|---|---|
| 1 | 2 | 3 | 4 | 5 | 6 | 7 | 8 | 9 | 10 |

| Get few of my sexual needs taken care of. | | | | | | Get most of my sexual needs taken care of. | | | |
|---|---|---|---|---|---|---|---|---|---|
| 1 | 2 | 3 | 4 | 5 | 6 | 7 | 8 | 9 | 10 |

| Think that my body is not very beautiful. | | | | | | Think that my body is very attractive. | | | |
|---|---|---|---|---|---|---|---|---|---|
| 1 | 2 | 3 | 4 | 5 | 6 | 7 | 8 | 9 | 10 |

Others find my body
very unattractive.

Others find my body
very attractive.

| 1 | 2 | 3 | 4 | 5 | 6 | 7 | 8 | 9 | 10 |

Must be in love
to really enjoy sex.

Can enjoy sex if I decide to;
doesn't depend on whether I am in love.

| 1 | 2 | 3 | 4 | 5 | 6 | 7 | 8 | 9 | 10 |

Usually find myself giving to others
sexually and doing what pleases them.

Find that I want to give and get
pleasure equally.

| 1 | 2 | 3 | 4 | 5 | 6 | 7 | 8 | 9 | 10 |

Often fake orgasms.

Never fake orgasms.

| 1 | 2 | 3 | 4 | 5 | 6 | 7 | 8 | 9 | 10 |

My sexual activity tends
to always be the same.

Like to engage in a variety
of sexual behaviors and activities.

| 1 | 2 | 3 | 4 | 5 | 6 | 7 | 8 | 9 | 10 |

Never masturbate.

Often masturbate.

| 1 | 2 | 3 | 4 | 5 | 6 | 7 | 8 | 9 | 10 |

Seldom or never have orgasms.

Usually have orgasms.

| 1 | 2 | 3 | 4 | 5 | 6 | 7 | 8 | 9 | 10 |

# Sexual Abuse

## *Exercise in Group Session: Drawing Safety*

Your facilitator will explain what this page is for.

# Exercise in Group Session: Self-Soothing Technique, Drawing Your Symbol or Souvenir

This page is blank so that you can draw your symbol or souvenir from the self-soothing exercise on it.

In your group session you received some clear definitions of sexual abuse:

- Whenever a child or adolescent is being used for the sexual stimulation of an adult, that is sexual abuse.
- Whenever an adult is being used for someone's sexual stimulation and he or she doesn't want to be used that way, that is sexual abuse.

Sexual behavior occurs on a continuum from thoughts and words to various kinds of touching to penetration. Sexuality involves our physical, emotional, social, and spiritual selves. It includes our perceptions and feelings about ourselves and others. It involves how we act and with whom we act.

Sexual abuse, like sexual behavior, occurs on a continuum. As you can see on the Sexual Abuse Continuum that follows, psychological abuse can include the "blurring of generational lines," in which daughters are treated like wives or sons are treated like husbands. It can involve an adult telling a child secrets about his or her sex life. It can be emotional abuse, in which an adult flirts, acts jealous, or in some other way manipulates a child's emotions. Covert sexual abuse includes inappropriate touching that appears accidental, a parent's habit of walking into the bathroom while a child or teenager is showering, or seductive comments about a child's developing body. Overt abuse involves kissing, displaying one's naked body to a child in order to get a sexual response, oral sex, and even penetration.

It's obviously more hurtful to be raped than to be teased, but any abuse can wound a woman's sense of self and sexuality. The damage includes

- Feeling that one is powerless and has no "say" in relationships
- Numbness during sex, inability to stay mentally present, fear of sex when clean and sober
- Lack of good judgment about relationships
- Reluctance to trust, fear of intimacy
- Shame about one's body and about being a woman

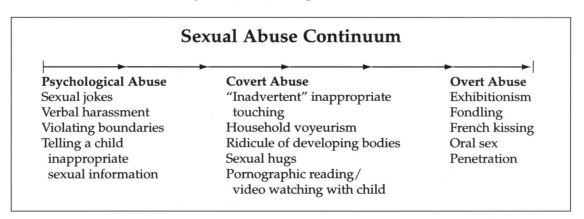

## Sexual Abuse Continuum

| Psychological Abuse | Covert Abuse | Overt Abuse |
|---|---|---|
| Sexual jokes | "Inadvertent" inappropriate touching | Exhibitionism |
| Verbal harassment | Household voyeurism | Fondling |
| Violating boundaries | Ridicule of developing bodies | French kissing |
| Telling a child inappropriate sexual information | Sexual hugs | Oral sex |
| | Pornographic reading/ video watching with child | Penetration |

# Reflections

1. What feelings did you have as a result of this session?

2. What issues did this session raise that you would like to discuss with your counselor? What questions about sexual abuse do you have?

3. You also talked about safety in the group session. You thought of an experience that made you feel comfortable and secure. Describe the comforting experience you thought of.

4. In the session, you also envisioned a symbol or souvenir to remind you of that comforting experience. What is the souvenir that you will use to remind you of the comforting experience whenever you feel anxious or upset?

5. Add your souvenir to your Self-Soothing Chart on page 54.

6. Finally, you talked a little about "necessary conditions." In preparation for our next session, think about what conditions you need in order to feel good about saying "yes" to sex. Here are some possibilities:

- You are clean and sober.
- Your partner is clean and sober.
- You are not too tired.
- Your body is free of significant pain.
- You are attracted to your partner.
- You know that your partner has no sexually transmitted diseases.
- You are using a condom.
- You are using some method of birth control.
- You are not afraid that your partner will judge your performance negatively.
- There is no unresolved tension between you and your partner.
- Your partner never abuses you emotionally, physically, or sexually.
- If you say no, your partner will accept it without punishing you physically or emotionally.
- Your partner cares about your pleasure as much as about his or her own.
- You are in a private place and will not be interrupted.

What are your necessary conditions? What do you need in order to feel safe and available sexually? (Even if you are living in a jail or prison, it is important to begin to think about what you need and want when you are released.)

# Fear of Sex
# While Clean and Sober

Most women who are in recovery are concerned about what it will be like to be sexual without the aid of alcohol or other drugs. Typically, the women have three fears:

- If they've never been sexual while clean and sober, they don't know what to expect or how they will respond. They're afraid of the unknown.
- They're afraid that sex without alcohol or drugs will be dissatisfying—that they are doomed to have no sex, not enough sex, or dissatisfying sex for the rest of their lives.
- They're simply afraid to have sex. Perhaps they have been using alcohol or drugs to cover up their fears of sex, but now they don't have anything to shield them from their fears.

These fears are normal. The more positive experiences you have with sex while clean and sober, the less anxious you will feel about it. Also, for women who have had healthy sexual lives, looking at sexuality during their recovery will enhance that satisfaction. Even if you are incarcerated now, this session will help you to think about issues that may be important to you when you are released.

# Reflections

1. One thing you can do to lessen your fear of sex when clean and sober is to make and maintain a Sexual Bill of Rights. Stating what you need in a relationship will help you to create a healthy, growth-fostering relationship. You discussed such a Sexual Bill of Rights in your group. Now make your own list of rights.

   As a sexual person, I have a right . . .

2. Read over your list of rights. Put a check mark beside each one that is not currently part of your sexual life. Why do you think that you don't have that right at this time? Why might you be afraid to have that right?

3. Visualize yourself having each of the rights on your list. What will you have to do to make each of them a reality in your life?

# Recovery Scale

Please take a few moments to mark the degree to which you do each of the following things. You assessed yourself like this at the beginning of this module on Sexuality. Please reassess yourself to see where you are now. You will not have to compare your answers with anyone else in the group, and no one will judge how well you are doing. This is not a test; it is an opportunity for you to chart your own progress in recovery.

If you are currently living in a correctional setting, some of the items may not be relevant at this time. You can cross them out or just not respond to them (but you may want to think about how you would like your life to be in the future, when you are released).

| | Not at All | Just a Little | Pretty Much | Very Much |
|---|---|---|---|---|
| 1. I know my body. | | | | |
| 2. I can talk to my counselor about sexual concerns. | | | | |
| 3. I can speak comfortably and appropriately about sex. | | | | |
| 4. I can keep my body safe. | | | | |
| 5. I accept my body. | | | | |
| 6. I can be affectionate with others. | | | | |
| 7. I am a sensual person. | | | | |
| 8. I can accept sexual pleasure from myself. | | | | |
| 9. I can accept sexual pleasure from my partner. | | | | |
| 10. I initiate making love. | | | | |
| 11. I can express my sexual desires to my partner. | | | | |
| 12. I enjoy making love. | | | | |

# Module D
# Spirituality

# What Is Spirituality?

In true spirituality, we connect personally with a force, power, or strength beyond ourselves. Some people call this God, some call it Allah, others call it something else. During this final module in the program and throughout your life, you will be able to make up your own mind about what you think God or the sacred is about.

Women often speak of their spirituality in terms of relationships and connections. They describe it in terms such as "oneness," "wholeness," "connection to the universe," "connection to the earth," "creativity," "belief in something greater than myself," and "trust in a higher or deeper part of myself." The Twelve Steps talk about a Power greater than ourselves and a God as we understand God to be. Women who have suffered from people who have abused power may be more comfortable thinking of God as something *deeper* rather than as a *higher* Power.

It is believed that all humans have an inborn desire for spirituality, for God or wholeness or connection. We have a spiritual void inside us that we are thirsty to have filled. We know that we want something more than just us. Our society often encourages us to look for that something in achievement, possessions, people's approval, a man, children, or alcohol and drugs. The desire for more is a good, normal thing to have. But what we need to do is to start looking for that something in a Power that is higher or deeper than ourselves or any kind of drug.

# Reflections

1. What does spirituality mean to you?

2. What questions do you have about spirituality that you might want to ask your counselor?

3. How do you think your substance abuse has affected the spiritual part of yourself?

4. What kind of spirituality or meaning in your life do you want or need? What are you thirsty for right now?

5. As you think about the spiritual part of you, what decision or action do you want to make in your life?

# Recovery Scale

Please take a few moments to mark the degree to which you do each of the following things. You will assess yourself like this at the beginning of this module on Spirituality, and again at the end. You will not have to compare your answers with anyone else in the group, and no one will judge how well you are doing. This is not a test; it is an opportunity for you to chart your own progress in recovery.

|  | Not at All | Just a Little | Pretty Much | Very Much |
|---|---|---|---|---|
| 1. I acknowledge my spiritual needs. | | | | |
| 2. I nurture my spiritual environment and life. | | | | |
| 3. I find comfort in my spiritual practices. | | | | |
| 4. I have a deepening relationship and connection with God. | | | | |
| 5. I feel connected with the life experiences of others. | | | | |
| 6. I respect the spiritual beliefs and practices of others. | | | | |
| 7. I am developing a daily contact with the spiritual through prayer or meditation. | | | | |
| 8. I listen to myself/my inner voice. | | | | |
| 9. I have a vision for my life. | | | | |
| 10. I live one day at a time. | | | | |
| 11. Recovery is part of my future. | | | | |
| 12. I am grateful for the life I have today. | | | | |

# Prayer and Meditation

Step Eleven of the Twelve Steps encourages us to establish "conscious contact" with our Higher Power. Your spiritual self is like a garden that needs to be watered and cared for if it is to grow. Step Eleven recommends meditation and prayer as ways to do this. Meditation is the practice of being still and focusing. It is a time to surrender, to let go, and to receive peace. In meditating, you give yourself permission to do nothing, without guilt. From the simple act of prayer or meditation, in doing nothing we find the wisdom and strength to go back and do what we need to do.

Meditation can help a person to find serenity. "Serenity is not freedom from the storms of life. It is the calm center that gets me through." We create this calm center through meditation.

You tried several meditation techniques in your group: breathing, walking, and focusing on an object from nature. They are summarized here.

**Breathing:** Sit in a quiet place, free from distractions. Empty your hands and lap, sit up straight, and place your feet flat on the floor. (If you prefer, you may sit on the floor.) Close your eyes (or focus your eyes on one object) and pay attention to the breath at the tip of your nose. Count to four slowly as you breathe in. Then count to four as you breathe out. Try to keep doing this for five minutes or so. If a thought comes into your mind, just acknowledge it and let it go. Then go back to focusing on your breathing.

**Walking:** Walk very slowly, focusing on how your body feels as it moves. Relax your breathing. Disregard whatever is around you. If a thought comes into your mind or you notice something outside you, just acknowledge it and let it go. Then focus again on your walking.

**Focusing on an Object from Nature:** Sit comfortably. Place your object on a table in front of you or hold it in your hand. Take five or ten minutes to look at it and really see it, feel it, experience it. Think about it, allowing all other thoughts to drift out of your mind.

Another way to meditate is to take a long, slow walk outdoors and fix your attention on what is around you. The best place to do this is in a peaceful place, not surrounded by noises. You also can sit in a peaceful place outdoors, such as a quiet yard or a park, or you can visit a chapel or library where you can focus on breathing slowly and observing the beautiful, peaceful things around you.

With any of these forms of meditation, it is important to let the concerns of the day and the thoughts that pop up pass through your mind without seizing your attention. If you find your mind wandering, just bring it back gently to whatever you are focusing on—your breath, your walking, or the object you are looking at. If feelings come up, observe them and let them go. Don't try to suppress them, just let your body feel them and then turn your attention back to your focus.

## Reflections

1. After you have tried at least one of these forms of meditation on your own, write down how it felt.

2. Was any part of it difficult? What might you do to make that less difficult in the future?

3. What did you like about it?

4. What did you feel in your body, if anything?

# Creating a Vision

This is the final session of this group. You have come a long way!

At the beginning of the program you took a retrospective journey: you looked *back* at the journey of your life from its beginning until you began the program. Now you will look *forward* in an exercise called the Prospective Journey. The Prospective Journey builds on what some people call the "promises of recovery" from Alcoholics Anonymous.[1] These are

> If we are painstaking about this phase of our development, we will be amazed before we are halfway through. We are going to know a new freedom and a new happiness. We will not regret the past nor wish to shut the door on it. We will comprehend the word serenity and we will know peace. No matter how far down the scale we have gone, we will see how our experience can benefit others. That feeling of uselessness and self-pity will disappear. We will lose interest in selfish things and gain interest in our fellows. Self-seeking will slip away. Our whole attitude and outlook upon life will change. Fear of people and of economic insecurity will leave us. We will intuitively know how to handle situations which used to baffle us. We will suddenly realize that God is doing for us what we could not do for ourselves.
>
> Are these extravagant promises? We think not. They are being fulfilled among us sometimes quickly, sometimes slowly. They will always materialize if we work for them.

---

[1] *Alcoholics Anonymous: The Story of How Many Thousands of Men and Women Have Recovered from Alcoholism* (3rd. ed.). New York: Alcoholics Anonymous World Services, Inc., 1976, pp. 83–84.

**113**

These "promises" are one of the spiritual tools that people in recovery have used for years in their spiritual growth. In the Appendix, you'll find some more spiritual tools, including

- Five Primary Practices of the Oxford Group
- The Twelve Steps of Alcoholics Anonymous
- A.A. Slogans
- The Serenity Prayer
- The Synanon Prayer

You'll also find alternatives to the Twelve Steps of A.A. These include

- The Sixteen Steps for Discovery and Empowerment (Charlotte Kasl)
- A New Version of the Twelve Steps (David Berenson)
- Thirteen Statements of Affirmation or Acceptance (Women for Sobriety)
- Save Our Selves/(SOS)/Secular Organization for Sobriety
- Rational Recovery

## *Exercise in Group Session: Prospective Journey*

On the next page is the following sentence with blanks in it.

> "It's now [six months from today], and as I look back over the last six months of my life, I see . . ."

In the first blank, write the date six months from today. The rest of this page gives you space in which to fill in what you see in your future. Imagine yourself six months from now, writing about where you are on that date and what the six-month journey has been like for you. You will be writing in the present tense as though you are already at that point in time. If you prefer not to write, you may draw pictures to show your journey and your life at that point.

## Prospective Journey

It's now _____, and as I look back over the last six months of my life, I see . . .

One of the last things you did in the group was to review the group experience using a process called ORID[2]. ORID stands for Objective-Reflective-Interpretive-Decisive. You can use the ORID method to process any experience. You may find it helpful to come back to this four-stage process whenever you have a decision to make or whenever you want to sort through a significant experience in your mind.

As you address these four stages during your group meeting, note your answers to the questions here:

**O** is for Objective

*What did you observe during the experience?*

*What are some of the things you remember doing, seeing, or hearing in the group?*

**R** is for Reflective

*What did you feel about the experience?*

*What were the high points of the group for you?*

*What were the low points?*

---

[2]"Elements of a Guided Discussion, ORID Model," from chapter 4, The ToP Focused Conversation Method, from *Winning Through Participation*, by Laura J. Spencer. Reprinted by permission of Kendall/Hunt Publishing Company.

**I** is for Interpretive

*What did you gain from the experience?*

*What was the greatest learning or insight you gained from this group?*

**D** is for Decisive

*What will you do in response to the experience?*

*What actions or decisions will you take to express your learning and growth?*

## Reflections

Look back at the "promises." These promises are for you. You have come a long way in your journey of recovery already, but your journey into a new kind of life is just beginning.

On your own, after the last group meeting, take a few minutes to think about your life since you began this program. What are you grateful for? (Gratitude is a spiritual practice that many people find helpful in their recovery.)

Congratulations on your work in this program and best wishes to you. May you have the serenity to accept the things you cannot change, the courage to change the things you can, and the wisdom to know the difference.

# Recovery Scale

Please take a few moments to mark the degree to which you do each of the following things. You assessed yourself like this at the beginning of this module on Spirituality. Please reassess yourself to see where you are now.

You may want to come back to these recovery scales as you progress on your journey, to see the progress that you have made.

| | Not at All | Just a Little | Pretty Much | Very Much |
|---|---|---|---|---|
| 1. I acknowledge my spiritual needs. | | | | |
| 2. I nurture my spiritual environment and life. | | | | |
| 3. I find comfort in my spiritual practices. | | | | |
| 4. I have a deepening relationship and connection with God. | | | | |
| 5. I feel connected with the life experiences of others. | | | | |
| 6. I respect the spiritual beliefs and practices of others. | | | | |
| 7. I am developing a daily contact with the spiritual through prayer or meditation. | | | | |
| 8. I listen to myself/my inner voice. | | | | |
| 9. I have a vision for my life. | | | | |
| 10. I live one day at a time. | | | | |
| 11. Recovery is part of my future. | | | | |
| 12. I am grateful for the life I have today. | | | | |

# Appendix: Additional Recovery Resources

# I. Five Primary Practices of the Oxford Group

The Oxford Group was a religious group that influenced the early development of Alcoholics Anonymous.

## 1. Confidence

Speaking truthfully

## 2. Confession

Saying the true and difficult things

## 3. Conviction

Having a sense of wrongdoing or guilt

## 4. Conversion

Acceptance of an altered way of life

## 5. Continuance

Helping others as you have been helped

# II. The Twelve Steps of Alcoholics Anonymous

Alcoholics Anonymous was founded in 1935 when two alcoholics joined together to share experiences, strengths, and hopes and found that this sharing enabled them to become and remain sober. They developed the A.A. program around the following Twelve Steps of recovery:

1. We admitted we were powerless over alcohol—that our lives had become unmanageable.

2. Came to believe that a Power greater than ourselves could restore us to sanity.

3. Made a decision to turn our will and our lives over to the care of God *as we understood Him.*

4. Made a searching and fearless moral inventory of ourselves.

5. Admitted to God, to ourselves, and to another human being the exact nature of our wrongs.

6. Were entirely ready to have God remove all these defects of character.

7. Humbly asked Him to remove our shortcomings.

8. Made a list of all persons we had harmed, and became willing to make amends to them all.

9. Made direct amends to such people wherever possible, except when to do so would injure them or others.

10. Continued to take personal inventory and when we were wrong promptly admitted it.

11. Sought through prayer and meditation to improve our conscious contact with God *as we understood Him,* praying only for knowledge of His will for us and the power to carry that out.

12. Having had a spiritual awakening as the result of these steps, we tried to carry this message to alcoholics, and to practice these principles in all our affairs.

---

# III. A.A. Slogans

Over the years, people in Alcoholics Anonymous have developed a number of slogans—simple phrases that people can easily remember and apply in practical ways every day. These are some of the slogans:

**One Day at a Time**

**Let Go and Let God**

**Keep It Simple**

**Keep Coming Back**

**Live and Let Live**

# IV. The Serenity Prayer

This prayer was first read aloud in a church service by Minister Reinhold Niebuhr in Heath, Massachusetts, in 1934. The actual author is unknown. A man who attended the church that day asked for a copy of the prayer. The minister wrote it down on a card and said that he had no further use for it. A member of A.A. found the prayer in an obituary column and showed it to Bill Wilson, the co-founder of A.A. The prayer has been used in A.A. meetings ever since.

> **God, grant me the serenity to accept**
> **the things I cannot change,**
> **The courage to change the things I can,**
> **And the wisdom to know the difference.**

# V. The Synanon Prayer

Synanon was founded by Chuck and Betty Dederich in 1958. Chuck Dederich was an alcoholic and a former Gulf Oil executive who wanted a more challenging and interactive approach to sobriety than A.A. provided. He began hosting A.A. meetings with more discussion (cross-talk, or responding to someone else's story with feedback, is discouraged in A.A. meetings). For economic reasons, recovering alcoholics began living together in what came to be called a "therapeutic community." In that community, the first heroin addicts entered recovery without medical help. Although Synanon no longer exists, therapeutic communities continue.

> **Please let me first and always examine myself.**
> **Let me be honest and truthful.**
> **Let me seek and assume responsibility.**
> **Let me understand rather than be understood.**
> **Let me trust and have faith in myself and my fellow man.**
> **Let me love rather than be loved.**
> **Let me give rather than receive.**

Excerpted from *Basic Interface* (Volume I), published by Amity, Inc., Tucson, AZ, 1994.

# VI. The Sixteen Steps for Discovery and Empowerment (Charlotte Kasl)

In *Many Roads, One Journey* (1991), Charlotte Kasl critiqued the Twelve Steps from a feminist perspective. Kasl thinks that the Twelve Step emphasis on powerlessness is unhelpful for women. She believes that many women drink or use drugs as a way of dealing with the lack of power in their lives. Her Sixteen Steps are designed as an alternative to the Twelve Steps.

1. We affirm we have the power to take charge of our lives and stop being dependent on substances or other people for our self-esteem and security. [*Alternative:* We admit/acknowledge we are out of control with/powerless over [fill in], yet have the power to take charge of our lives and stop being dependent on substances or other people for our self-esteem and security.]

2. We come to believe that God/Goddess/Universe/Great Spirit/Higher Power awakens the healing wisdom within us when we open ourselves to that power.

3. We make a decision to become our authentic selves and trust in the healing power of the truth.

4. We examine our beliefs, addictions, and dependent behavior in the context of living in a hierarchical, patriarchal culture.

5. We share with another person and the Universe all those things inside of us for which we feel shame and guilt.

6. We appreciate and develop our intelligence, strengths, and creativity, remembering not to hide these qualities from ourselves and others.

7. We become willing to let go of shame, guilt, and any behavior that keeps us from loving ourselves and others.

8. We make a list of people we have harmed and people who have harmed us, and take steps to clear out negative energy by making amends and sharing our grievances in a respectful way.

9. We express love and gratitude to others, and increasingly appreciate the wonder of life and the blessings we do have.

10. We learn to trust our reality and daily affirm that we see what we see, we know what we know, and we feel what we feel.

11. We promptly admit to mistakes and make amends when appropriate, but we do not say we are sorry for things we have not done and we do not cover up, analyze, or take responsibility for the shortcomings of others.

12. We seek out situations, jobs, and people that affirm our intelligence, perceptions, and self-worth and avoid situations or people who are hurtful, harmful, or demeaning to us.

13. We take steps to heal our physical bodies, organize our lives, reduce stress, and have fun.

14. We seek to find our inward calling, and develop the will and wisdom to follow it.

15. We accept the ups and downs of life as natural events that can be used as lessons for our growth.

16. We grow in awareness that we are sacred beings, interrelated with all living things, and we contribute to restoring peace and balance on the planet.

---

Reprinted with permission from *Many Roads, One Journey: Moving Beyond the Twelve Steps.* New York: HarperCollins, 1992. Copyright © Charlotte Kasl, 1991/1993.

# VII. A New Version of the Twelve Steps (David Berenson)

In 1991, David Berenson proposed this new version of the Twelve Steps in response to the critiques from feminists. He aims to retain the essence of the Twelve Steps while expressing them in language that he thinks may be more valid fifty years after they were first formulated.

1. Admitted that we have a problem and recognized that our social environment contributes to our problem.

2. Recognized that help is available and that there are other ways of coping.

3. Became willing to change and asked for help.

4. Looked at both our healthy and unhealthy behaviors and coping skills.

5. Broke the silence—shared our lives, our pain, and our joy with others.

6. Became teachable; became willing to learn new healthy behaviors to replace our unhealthy behaviors.

7. Began to forgive ourselves and others.

8. Became aware of and accepted responsibility for the harm we caused ourselves and others, recognizing that we do not need to take responsibility for those who harmed us.

9. Did what we could, without harming ourselves or others, to repair these damages and not repeat the unhealthy behavior.

10. Took responsibility for our day-to-day behavior, recognizing both our healthy and unhealthy behaviors.

11. Developed our individual spirituality, seeking inner wisdom and strength.

12. As a result of ongoing healing and growth, we tried to live happier, healthier lives; learning to love and accept ourselves as we are; sharing our recovery with others.

---

Reprinted with permission from "Powerlessness—Liberating or Enslaving? Responding to the Feminist Critique of the Twelve Steps," by David Berenson, in *Feminism and Addiction*, C. Bepko (Ed.). New York: Haworth Press, Inc., 1991.

# VIII. Thirteen Statements of Affirmation or Acceptance (Women for Sobriety)

Founded in 1972, Women for Sobriety (WFS) resembles a traditional feminist consciousness-raising group, where women talk about their lives from a distinctly female perspective. WFS focuses on women and emphasizes the value of each woman. Instead of the Twelve Steps, WFS groups use the following thirteen steps:

1. I have a life-threatening problem that once had me.
2. Negative thoughts destroy only myself.
3. Happiness is a habit I will develop.
4. Problems bother me only to the degree I permit them to.
5. I am what I think.
6. Life can be ordinary or it can be great.
7. Love can change the course of my world.
8. The fundamental object of life is emotional and spiritual growth.
9. The past is gone forever.
10. All love given returns.
11. Enthusiasm is my daily exercise.
12. I am a competent woman and have much to give life.
13. I am responsible for myself and my actions.

Reprinted with permission from: Women for Sobriety, Founder, Dr. Jean Kirkpatrick. Copyright © Women for Sobriety, Inc., P.O. Box 618, Quakertown, PA 18951-0618.

# IX. Save Our Selves/(SOS)/Secular Organization for Sobriety

Founded in 1986, SOS addresses the needs of atheistic, agnostic, and humanistic alcoholics who like much of the program and format of A.A. but who prefer not to deal with a Higher Power in any form.

SOS
5521 Grosvenor Boulevard
Los Angeles, CA 90066
Telephone: (310) 821-8430
Fax: (310) 821-2610

# X. Rational Recovery

Rational Recovery is the concept of immediate self-recovery through planned abstinence put into practice by using an easily learned thinking skill called Addictive Voice Recognition Technique® (AVRT).

Rational Recovery Systems, Inc.
Box 800
Lotus, CA 95651
Telephone: (530) 621-4374
Web page: http://www.rational.org/recovery/

# Feedback Form

Dear Recovering Woman:

I would appreciate hearing about your experience with the *Helping Women Recover* program. Any information you would like to share with me will be greatly appreciated.

Describe yourself:

Describe where you participated in this program:

Your experience with the *Helping Women Recover* program:

What did you find most useful?

Why? How?

What did you find least useful?

Why? How?

Other suggestions/comments:

Thank you for your input.

Please return this form to:
        Stephanie S. Covington, Ph.D.
        Institute for Relational Development
        7946 Ivanhoe Avenue, Suite 201B
        La Jolla, CA 92037
        Fax: (858) 454-8598
        E-mail: sscird@aol.com